FINCASTLE LIBRARY
11 Academy Street
P.O. Box 129
Fincastle, VA 24090

POINTS OF VIEW

Should BULLYING Be a Crime?

By Emma Jones

KidHaven PUBLISHING

Botetourt County Library

Published in 2020 by
KidHaven Publishing, an Imprint of Greenhaven Publishing, LLC
353 3rd Avenue
Suite 255
New York, NY 10010

Copyright © 2020 KidHaven Publishing, an Imprint of Greenhaven Publishing, LLC.

All rights reserved. No part of this book may be reproduced in any form without permission in writing from the publisher, except by a reviewer.

Designer: Deanna Paternostro
Editor: Katie Kawa

Photo credits: Cover SpeedKingz/Shutterstock.com; p. 5 (top) wavebreakmedia/Shutterstock.com; p. 5 (bottom) Robert Kneschke/Shutterstock.com; pp. 7 (top), 9 (top), 19 Monkey Business Images/Shutterstock.com; p. 7 (bottom) Kate Way/Shutterstock.com; pp. 9 (bottom), 21 (inset, middle) Daisy Daisy/Shutterstock.com; p. 11 Potstock/Shutterstock.com; p. 13 Kamira/Shutterstock.com; p. 15 Kayasit Sonsupap/Shutterstock.com; p. 17 Dmytro Zinkevych/Shutterstock.com; p. 21 (notepad) ESB Professional/Shutterstock.com; p. 21 (markers) Kucher Serhii/Shutterstock.com; p. 21 (photo frame) FARBAI/iStock/Thinkstock; p. 21 (inset, left) fizkes/Shutterstock.com; p. 21 (inset, right) Pixel-Shot/Shutterstock.com.

Cataloging-in-Publication Data

Names: Jones, Emma.
Title: Should bullying be a crime? / Emma Jones.
Description: New York : KidHaven Publishing, 2020. | Series: Points of view | Includes glossary and index.
Identifiers: ISBN 9781534532076 (pbk.) | ISBN 9781534531956 (library bound) | ISBN 9781534532137 (6 pack) | ISBN 9781534532014 (ebook)
Subjects: LCSH: Bullying–Juvenile literature. | Bullying–Prevention–Juvenile literature. | Cyberbullying–Juvenile literature. | Victims of bullying–Juvenile literature.
Classification: LCC BF637.B85 J66 2020 | DDC 302.34'3–dc23

Printed in the United States of America

Some of the images in this book illustrate individuals who are models. The depictions do not imply actual situations or events.

CPSIA compliance information: Batch #BW20KL: For further information contact Greenhaven Publishing LLC, New York, New York at 1-844-317-7404.

Please visit our website, www.greenhavenpublishing.com. For a free color catalog of all our high-quality books, call toll free 1-844-317-7404 or fax 1-844-317-7405.

CONTENTS

A Big Problem 4
Different Laws 6
When Is It Already a Crime? 8
Private and Personal 10
Serious Effects 12
A New Set of Problems 14
Parents Pay the Price 16
Prevention or Punishment? 18
Strong Feelings 20
Glossary 22
For More Information 23
Index 24

A Big PROBLEM

Most people agree that bullying is a big problem. However, different people have different points of view about how to solve, or fix, this problem. One idea is to make bullying a crime, which means bullies—and sometimes their parents or guardians—could be **punished** by having to pay fines or spend time in jail. Some people believe this could help stop bullying, but other people believe it could cause more problems.

Do you think bullying should be a crime? Before you decide, it's helpful to learn all the facts so you can have an informed, or educated, opinion.

Know the Facts!

Bullying can happen online too. Cyberbullying is the use of smartphones, computers, or other **devices** to send hurtful messages or share harmful posts about another person online.

Most people want to keep kids healthy, happy, and safe. They just have different ideas about how to do it.

Different LAWS

In the United States, there are many kinds of laws. Federal laws apply to the whole country because they come from the national government. State and local laws apply to smaller groups of people.

Because there's no federal law against bullying, states and local governments have come up with their own anti-bullying laws. Some of these laws require schools to report and deal with bullying when it happens. Other laws have set up **programs** to prevent bullying, or stop it before it starts. In some cases, laws have made certain kinds of bullying, such as cyberbullying, a crime.

Know the Facts!

All 50 U.S. states have passed laws that address bullying.

Different parts of the United States each have their own anti-bullying laws. This has led to many **debates** about which kinds of laws work best to stop bullying.

When Is It Already A CRIME?

Bullying can take many different forms and can happen for many different reasons. Certain kinds of bullying are already considered crimes because of how and why they happen. For example, some bullies use violence, or harm done to a person's body. Those actions can be considered a crime. Even if the **victim** doesn't actually get hurt, the bully can still be punished.

Bullies also often threaten people with violence, which means they make their victims think they're going to hurt them. Making true threats of violence is a crime. This includes threats made in person, through text messages, or online.

Know the Facts!

The federal government has laws that **protect** people from being bullied because of their race, their belief system, their sex, any disabilities they may have, or the country they come from. If bullying is happening for these reasons, schools are required by law to stop it.

If a bully is threatening to hurt you or someone you know, talk to a trusted adult. This kind of bullying is against the law, and it's important to get help from school officials and the police.

Private and PERSONAL

Violence and threats of violence aren't the only actions that are considered bullying. Spreading harmful lies about people, saying hurtful things to them, and keeping them out of a group on purpose are all examples of bullying too.

Some people think these things should also be considered crimes. Others believe these actions aren't as harmful as violence, so they shouldn't be treated the same way. They don't think someone who calls a person names should pay a fine or go to jail. They see this kind of bullying as something schools should handle instead of the police.

Know the Facts!

In order for an action to be considered bullying, it must be intentional—the bully must mean to do it to cause harm—and repetitive, which means there must be a pattern of harmful actions over a period of time. The bully must also be in a position of power over their victim.

Some people see bullying as a private and personal issue for parents and school officials to deal with instead of the government.

Serious EFFECTS

People who support making bullying a crime—also known as criminalizing bullying—believe that all bullying is **serious** and dangerous, or harmful. Children who are bullied are more likely to have **mental** health problems and sleep problems. Victims of bullying are also more likely to do poorly in school because of the problems they're facing. They might even drop out of school because they can't deal with the bullying anymore.

Many people think these serious effects call for serious **consequences** for bullies. They believe people who cause this kind of lasting harm should be charged with a crime.

Know the Facts!

One common mental health problem for victims of bullying is anxiety, which is a state of very strong worry that makes it hard to deal with daily life. Another is depression. Someone with depression generally feels sad, hopeless, or empty and has no interest in things they once enjoyed.

People who believe bullying should be a crime are often adults who've watched their children deal with the harmful effects of bullying.

A New Set of PROBLEMS

People who oppose making all bullying a crime argue that putting bullies in jail isn't the **solution** because it just creates a new set of harmful effects. If a young person is put in jail, it starts a cycle that's hard to get out of, and they often end up back in jail after they get out. They also face problems finishing school.

Jails in the United States are already too crowded, and putting bullies in jail would only make that problem worse. Many people believe there are better ways to help bullies than putting them in jail.

Know the Facts!

Some bullies are also victims of bullying. They have a higher chance of having mental health problems than people who are only victims or only bullies.

Going to jail for a crime can follow a person for the rest of their life. Some people argue that sending bullies to jail would cause more problems than it would solve.

Parents Pay the PRICE

Some communities have passed laws that punish the parents or guardians of children who are caught bullying. In these communities, bullying is a crime, but after a warning, the parents or guardians of bullies are the ones who must pay a fine or go to jail.

Some people argue that parents shouldn't be **responsible** for what their children do, and many parents of bullies try to stop their child's bad behavior, or actions, without a formal warning. However, supporters of these kinds of laws believe they make adults take a more active role in ending their child's bullying.

Know the Facts!

More than 20 percent of students in the United States have been bullied at some point in their lives.

If parents face jail time for their child's actions, it might make them more likely to do something to help their child. For example, they might meet with school officials or take their child to a therapist—someone who helps people work through their problems.

Prevention or PUNISHMENT?

Bullying is a public health problem, which means it's an issue that **affects** the health of many people in a community. Some people are trying to treat bullying like they'd treat another health problem, which is by working to prevent it instead of criminalizing it. These people argue that making bullying a crime won't stop it. Punishment deals only with actions that have already happened instead of preventing them from happening in the first place.

Opponents of criminalizing bullying believe it doesn't get to the real cause of the problem. Punishment doesn't help a bully learn or become a better person.

Know the Facts!

A leading group of doctors in the United States wrote that it wouldn't be helpful to make bullying a crime. These doctors stated that schools should make their own policies, or rules, to prevent and address bullying.

Many people think the best way to deal with bullying is by stopping it before it starts. They believe teaching young kids to deal with their feelings in a healthy way and treat each other with respect is the first step to stopping bullying.

Strong
FEELINGS

Some people believe bullying is simply a part of growing up, but most people disagree. They want to do whatever they can to stop bullying and to help kids feel safe, loved, and welcome at school. Bullying is often a very personal issue, and that's why people have such strong feelings about how to stop it.

When someone has strong feelings about an issue, it can be hard for them to understand other points of view. However, it's never okay to bully someone or treat them poorly for having a different opinion. It's important to treat everyone with respect.

Know the Facts!

Adults deal with bullying too. In fact, more than 30 percent of Americans have said they've been bullied as adults. Adults are often bullied at work.

Should bullying be a crime?

YES

- Some actions taken by bullies are already illegal.

- Bullying causes serious problems that call for serious punishment.

- Punishing the parents of bullies can help them take action to stop their child's bullying.

- People should do whatever it takes to help kids feel safe in school.

NO

- Most bullying isn't serious enough to be a crime and should be handled by parents or school officials instead of the police.

- Sending a bully to jail causes more problems than it solves.

- Parents shouldn't be put in jail or fined for their child's actions because they're not the ones doing the bullying.

- Prevention is more helpful than punishment because punishment doesn't deal with the cause of the problem.

You can use this chart to help you compare different points of view about how to handle bullying. After learning the facts and ideas on both sides of the debate, what do you think? Should bullying be a crime?

GLOSSARY

affect: To produce an effect on something.

consequence: Something important that happens because of an action or set of conditions.

debate: An argument or discussion about an issue, generally between two sides.

device: A tool used for a certain purpose.

mental: Relating to the mind.

program: A plan under which action may be taken toward a goal.

protect: To keep safe.

punish: To make someone suffer for doing something wrong.

responsible: Getting the credit or blame for actions or decisions.

serious: Causing worry or harm.

solution: A correct answer to a problem.

victim: A person who is hurt by someone else.

For More INFORMATION

WEBSITES

Kids Talk About: Bullying (Video)
kidshealth.org/en/kids/talkabout-bullying.html
This video from the KidsHealth website features kids sharing their real stories of dealing with bullying.

StopBullying.gov: What Kids Can Do
www.stopbullying.gov/kids/what-you-can-do/index.html
This website offers tips for kids on how to handle bullying, including cyberbullying.

BOOKS

Miller, Connie Colwell. *You Can Stop Bullying: Stand by or Stand Up?*. Mankato, MN: Amicus Ink, 2019.

Murphy, Frank. *Stand Up to Bullying*. Ann Arbor, MI: Cherry Lake Publishing, 2019.

Pettiford, Rebecca. *Resisting Bullying*. Minneapolis, MN: Bullfrog Books, 2018.

Publisher's note to educators and parents: Our editors have carefully reviewed these websites to ensure that they are suitable for students. Many websites change frequently, however, and we cannot guarantee that a site's future contents will continue to meet our high standards of quality and educational value. Be advised that students should be closely supervised whenever they access the Internet.

INDEX

A
adult bullying, 20
anxiety, 12

C
criminalizing, 12, 18
cyberbullying, 4, 6

D
depression, 12
doctors, 18

F
fines, 4, 10, 16, 21

G
government, 6, 8, 11

J
jail, 4, 10, 14, 15, 16, 17, 21

L
laws, 6, 7, 8, 9, 16

M
mental health, 12, 14

P
parents, 4, 11, 16, 17, 21
police, 9, 10, 21
prevention, 6, 18, 21

R
respect, 19, 20

S
schools, 6, 8, 9, 10, 11, 12, 14, 17, 18, 20, 21

T
therapists, 17
threats, 8, 9, 10

V
victims, 8, 10, 12, 14
violence, 8, 10